The Thrill of Fear

250 Years of Scary Entertainment

Walter Kendrick

GROVE WEIDENFELD

New York

Published by Grove Weidenfeld
A division of Grove Press, Inc.
841 Broadway
New York, NY 10003-4793

Published in Canada by General Publishing Company, Ltd.

Library of Congress Cataloging-in-Publication Data

Kendrick, Walter M.
The thrill of fear : 250 years of scary entertainment / Walter Kendrick.—1st ed.
        p.   cm.
Includes bibliographical references.
ISBN 0-8021-1162-9
1. Horror tales, English—History and criticism.   2. Horror tales, American—History and criticism.   3. Popular literature—History and criticism.   4. Horror films—History and criticism.   5. Horror in literature.   6. Death in literature.   7. Amusements—History.
        I. Title.
PR830.T3K4   1991
823′.0873809—dc20   91-11495
                                          CIP

Manufactured in the United States of America

Printed on acid-free paper

Designed by Irving Perkins Associates

First Edition 1991

1   3   5   7   9   10   8   6   4   2

For M.

Acknowledgments

Many friends and colleagues helped me write this book—reading drafts, suggesting sources, letting their ideas bump heads with mine. For these and other kindnesses, I owe special thanks to Dan Applebaum, Aileen Baumgartner, Walt Bode, Flip Brophy, Karen Burke, Mark Caldwell, Robert Cornfield, Mary Erler, Michael Feingold, Richard Goldstein, Connie Hassett, Mary Anne Kowaleski, M. Mark, Rebecca Martin, Perry Meisel, Erika Munk, Art Murray, Debra Pearl, Lloyd Rose, Dave Sanjek, Ralph Sassone, Larry Stempel, and Joan Ungaro.

Thanks also to the staffs of the Fordham University and New York University libraries for their unfailing generosity and assistance.

Unless otherwise indicated in the source notes, all translations are my own.

Contents

Introduction: Fear Is the Same

With all or almost all animals, even with birds, Terror causes the body to tremble. The skin becomes pale, sweat breaks out, and the hair bristles. The secretions of the alimentary canal and of the kidneys are increased, and they are involuntarily voided. . . . The breathing is hurried. The heart beats quickly, wildly, and violently; but whether it pumps the blood more efficiently through the body may be doubted, for the surface seems bloodless and the strength of the muscles soon fails. . . . The mental faculties are much disturbed. Utter prostration soon follows, and even fainting. . . . I once caught a robin in a room, which fainted so completely, that for a time I thought it dead.

These were the symptoms of terror in 1872, as Charles Darwin described them in *The Expression of the Emotions in Man and Animals.* More than a century later, though the world is vastly different, terror hasn't changed. Birds, cats, dogs, and people, when they are frightened, continue to tremble, break out in cold sweats, and faint dead away. Whatever name you give it—fear, fright, terror, horror—the emotion may vary in intensity but remains in essence the same. You may not understand a syllable of a man's language; his customs may be wholly foreign to you; but when his eyes widen, his mouth hangs open, and his hands uncontrollably shake, you can read fear written all over him. The language seems universal among human beings; it also links us to animals, reminding us of our kinship with them. And we can assume that, ten thousand years ago, our remote ancestors joined us in feeling their hair stand on end when they were afraid. In all ages, nations, and even species, fear is the same.

Darwin speculated that fear's instinctual symptoms evolved, like all other features of life, because they aided survival. Fear was a response to some threat in the environment, especially to the approach of a predator. Standing hairs, for instance—or "the erection of the dermal appendages"—may make a threatened creature look "larger and more terrible to its enemies or rivals." An animal that exhibits such behavior would be more likely to win a mate and to escape being eaten; the trait would then be passed on to later, better-adapted generations. Even an apparently self-defeating maneuver like passing out cold can be accounted for in Darwin's view, because some carnivores will not bite an animal that seems dead already. Animals that play dead—as several species do—avoid real death by faking it.

The Expression of the Emotions is still a primary source for behavioral scientists, who still study the relation between animals' behavior and what they presumably feel. Nowadays, "piloerection" replaces both Darwin's clumsy "erection of the dermal appendages" and the more homely "goose-skin," as he occasionally called fear's characteristic prickle. But the phenomenon endures, and science goes on probing it—to small effect as far as I can see. Scientists freely admit that though we know fear when we feel it or see its symptoms, we may never be able to measure it precisely or mark it off clearly from the spectrum of emotions to which it belongs. Uncertainty grows when we consider the varieties of fear, from mild anxiety to out-and-out terror, for which we also have words. Like "fear" itself, these words do not guarantee the existence of any identifiable condition of body or mind. They blend into one another; one man's frisson may be another man's stark horror or a third man's occasion for belly laughs.

In human beings (whom most of us find more compelling than robins), the body may do what animals do, but the mind is likely to be otherwise engaged. Discussing the erection of the hair, Darwin cited a case reported to him by Dr. J. Crichton Browne, the head of a large insane asylum:

> For instance, it is occasionally necessary to inject morphia under the skin of an insane woman, who dreads the operation extremely, though it causes very little pain; for she believes that poison is being introduced into her system, and that her bones will be softened, and her flesh turned into dust. She becomes deadly pale; her limbs are stiffened by a sort of tetanic spasm, and her hair is partially erected on the front of the head.

The symptoms were plainly those of intense fear, which sufficed for Darwin's purposes. He therefore passed over the most human aspect of the poor woman's case. She was terrified, just as a cat or a bird might be, yet her fear had no object or at best a wholly imaginary one. What frightened her was not so much the morphine or even the needle as a vision that only she could see, the spectacle of her body rotting away.

Neither Darwin nor Dr. Crichton Browne disputed the power of such a vision to bring on the symptoms of terror. There was nothing insane about the woman's response; madness lay in the lack of correspondence between her imagination and reality. A couple of centuries earlier, any preacher might have informed the learned gentlemen that their inmate was wiser than they. Her mistake was merely to suppose that morphine and needles would do the trick; nothing so drastic, only time, was required. Her bones indeed would soften; her flesh would turn to dust; so would the learned gentlemen's, for that matter. They would all die, in whatever way, at whatever moment, inevitably. The preacher might have urged the scientist and the doctor to heed the woman's vision, instead of calling it madness or gauging what it did to her hair. She glimpsed eternal truth; they saw mere phenomena.

It has often been said—though a proper survey remains to be taken—that human beings are the only species who know they must die, who can conjure up the event as if it were happening now and react accordingly. Animals fear death, but the fear seems to come on them only when death immediately threatens. They do not brood upon it; for animals, death is an endemic surprise. Dr. Crichton Browne's madwoman reminds us that human beings can also imagine being dead, a very different thing from death and perhaps a more frightening one. Deprived of soul, spirit, force, whatever you may call it (this fear requires no religion), human flesh is meat, and it goes meat's way. Few seventeenth-century preachers would have balked at summoning up the madwoman's vision in their congregations' minds. Then, as in all prior Christian centuries, the lesson was plain and familiar: Put your faith in flesh and you'll end up feeding worms; put your faith in spirit, subdue the ephemeral flesh, and you'll transcend the grave.

Well into the eighteenth century such lessons went on being preached, but they sharply dwindled after 1750, and I know of no one who preaches in that style now. By 1872, the idea that the flesh will rot seemed as horrifying as ever, to mad and sane alike. The idea, however, had long since lost its religious usefulness; though it could still frighten, it no longer admonished. Indeed, decorum hardly admitted notions of deadness into public discourse. Fond as they were of funerals and all the panoply of mourning, the Victorians exhibited a thoroughly modern squeamishness in regard to the symptoms of being dead. They continued a development that began at the end of the seventeenth century and has not ceased—hiding deadness away, cosmeticizing corpses, denying ever more strenuously that anything nasty happens to the body after death. The gaudy American funeral industry that Evelyn Waugh lampooned in *The Loved One* (1948) and Jessica Mitford lambasted in *The American Way of Death* (1963) is only the most grotesque by-product of a long, slow, immensely complex process of deliberate forgetting.

It may seem paradoxical that death itself, especially violent death, has remained immune to the taboo against deadness. In their newspapers, melodramas, and popular fiction, the Victorians exhibited the same fervent interest in the varieties of dying that their Elizabethan and Jacobean ancestors had gratified at bloody stage plays and public executions. We have inherited that interest, and we cultivate it, if possible, with even greater fervor. But our interest fades once the deed is done; what happens to the corpse thereafter belongs in a different zone, a shadowy one, where we, like the Victorians, would prefer not to tread. Those Elizabethans and Jacobeans (and the generations before them) exhibited a very different attitude, one that must strike a modern observer as callous, revolting, utterly incomprehensible, or perhaps all three. Before the

Introduction:
fear Is the Same

With all or almost all animals, even with birds, Terror causes the body to tremble. The skin becomes pale, sweat breaks out, and the hair bristles. The secretions of the alimentary canal and of the kidneys are increased, and they are involuntarily voided. . . . The breathing is hurried. The heart beats quickly, wildly, and violently; but whether it pumps the blood more efficiently through the body may be doubted, for the surface seems bloodless and the strength of the muscles soon fails. . . . The mental faculties are much disturbed. Utter prostration soon follows, and even fainting. . . . I once caught a robin in a room, which fainted so completely, that for a time I thought it dead.

These were the symptoms of terror in 1872, as Charles Darwin described them in *The Expression of the Emotions in Man and Animals*. More than a century later, though the world is vastly different, terror hasn't changed. Birds, cats, dogs, and people, when they are frightened, continue to tremble, break out in cold sweats, and faint dead away. Whatever name you give it—fear, fright, terror, horror—the emotion may vary in intensity but remains in essence the same. You may not understand a syllable of a man's language; his customs may be wholly foreign to you; but when his eyes widen, his mouth hangs open, and his hands uncontrollably shake, you can read fear written all over him. The language seems universal among human beings; it also links us to animals, reminding us of our kinship with them. And we can assume that, ten thousand years ago, our remote ancestors joined us in feeling their hair stand on end when they were afraid. In all ages, nations, and even species, fear is the same.

Darwin speculated that fear's instinctual symptoms evolved, like all other features of life, because they aided survival. Fear was a response to some threat in the environment, especially to the approach of a predator. Standing hairs, for instance—or "the erection of the dermal appendages"—may make a threatened creature look "larger and more terrible to its enemies or rivals." An animal that exhibits such behavior would be more likely to win a mate and to escape being eaten; the trait would then be passed on to later, better-adapted generations. Even an apparently self-defeating maneuver like passing out cold can be accounted for in Darwin's view, because some carnivores will not bite an animal that seems dead already. Animals that play dead—as several species do—avoid real death by faking it.

The Expression of the Emotions is still a primary source for behavioral scientists, who still study the relation between animals' behavior and what they presumably feel. Nowadays, "piloerection" replaces both Darwin's clumsy "erection of the dermal appendages" and the more homely "goose-skin," as he occasionally called fear's characteristic prickle. But the phenomenon endures, and science goes on probing it—to small effect as far as I can see. Scientists freely admit that though we know fear when we feel it or see its symptoms, we may never be able to measure it precisely or mark it off clearly from the spectrum of emotions to which it belongs. Uncertainty grows when we consider the varieties of fear, from mild anxiety to out-and-out terror, for which we also have words. Like "fear" itself, these words do not guarantee the existence of any identifiable condition of body or mind. They blend into one another; one man's frisson may be another man's stark horror or a third man's occasion for belly laughs.

In human beings (whom most of us find more compelling than robins), the body may do what animals do, but the mind is likely to